HAL•LEONARD
INSTRUMENTAL PLAY-ALONG

CLARINET

Disney CLASSICS

T0083897

THE CD IS PLAYABLE ON ANY CD PLAYER. FOR PC AND MAC USERS, THE CD IS ENHANCED
SO YOU CAN ADJUST THE RECORDING TO ANY TEMPO WITHOUT CHANGING PITCH.

The following songs are the property of:
BOURNE CO.
Music Publishers
5 West 37th Street
New York, NY 10018

Baby Mine
Give a Little Whistle
Heigh-Ho
I've Got No Strings

Some Day My Prince Will Come
When You Wish Upon a Star
Whistle While You Work
Who's Afraid of the Big Bad Wolf?

Disney characters and artwork © Disney Enterprises, Inc.

ISBN 978-1-4584-1597-4

WALT DISNEY MUSIC COMPANY
WONDERLAND MUSIC COMPANY, INC.

DISTRIBUTED BY

HAL•LEONARD®
CORPORATION
7777 W. BLUEMOUND RD. P.O. BOX 13819 MILWAUKEE, WI 53213

Visit Hal Leonard Online at
www.halleonard.com

ALICE IN WONDERLAND

from Walt Disney's ALICE IN WONDERLAND

Words by BOB HILLIARD
Music by SAMMY FAIN

CLARINET

BABY MINE

from Walt Disney's DUMBO

CLARINET

Words by NED WASHINGTON
Music by FRANK CHURCHILL

3/4

BELLA NOTTE

(This Is the Night)

from Walt Disney's LADY AND THE TRAMP

Words and Music by PEGGY LEE
and SONNY BURKE

GIVE A LITTLE WHISTLE

from Walt Disney's PINOCCHIO

7/8

CLARINET

Words by NED WASHINGTON
Music by LEIGH HARLINE

HEIGH-HO

The Dwarfs' Marching Song from Walt Disney's SNOW WHITE AND THE SEVEN DWARFS

9/10

CLARINET

Words by LARRY MOREY
Music by FRANK CHURCHILL

I'VE GOT NO STRINGS

from Walt Disney's PINOCCHIO

CLARINET

Words by NED WASHINGTON
Music by LEIGH HARLINE

LITTLE APRIL SHOWER

from Walt Disney's BAMBI

Words by LARRY MOREY
Music by FRANK CHURCHILL

13/14

CLARINET

ONCE UPON A DREAM
from Walt Disney's SLEEPING BEAUTY

CLARINET

Words and Music by SAMMY FAIN
and JACK LAWRENCE
Adapted from a Theme by Tchaikovsky

rit.

SOME DAY MY PRINCE WILL COME

from Walt Disney's SNOW WHITE AND THE SEVEN DWARFS

17/18

CLARINET

Words by LARRY MOREY
Music by FRANK CHURCHILL

THE UNBIRTHDAY SONG
from Walt Disney's ALICE IN WONDERLAND

19/20

CLARINET

Words and Music by MACK DAVID,
AL HOFFMAN and JERRY LIVINGSTON

WHEN YOU WISH UPON A STAR

from Walt Disney's PINOCCHIO

21/22

CLARINET

Words by NED WASHINGTON
Music by LEIGH HARLINE

WHISTLE WHILE YOU WORK

from Walt Disney's SNOW WHITE AND THE SEVEN DWARFS

Words by LARRY MOREY
Music by FRANK CHURCHILL

CLARINET

WHO'S AFRAID OF THE BIG BAD WOLF?

from Walt Disney's THREE LITTLE PIGS

25/26

CLARINET

Words and Music by FRANK CHURCHILL
Additional Lyric by ANN RONELL

Moderately

YOU CAN FLY! YOU CAN FLY! YOU CAN FLY!

from Walt Disney's PETER PAN

Words by SAMMY CAHN
Music by SAMMY FAIN

27/28
CLARINET